An Antho...
Word, Sound and
Power.

written by
Ras Slywayne

TABLE OF CONTENTS

TABLE OF CONTENTS

An Ability

It's that feeling...
Your heart's pounding you feel it in your chest
As if it were to burst through your rib
Is this Love?

Or is love a mere feeling of enjoyment for
someone, sexual attraction or infatuation.

What is it when you feel this way?
Can't stop thinking about this person
Your soul's recognition of its counterpoint
And you know this meticulous person, would
make you a better version of yourself...

I don't know what the future holds for me, but where ever I end up, I'll make the best of it, I'll be happy, since there is true guarantee of tomorrow...

Hence I say
Love is not a feeling
Its an ability

Are you able to Love???

Awestruck

I recognized a sound; a spasm of what might have been dismay or disgust crossed my seldom pale face.

What was this sound? I asked myself, it was the sound of nothing.

I then became too overwrought to even sleep, I had to escape from this sound or I might succumb to the urge to scream and throw things.

Then without a warning sign I crashed, I collided with someone extraordinary.

My breath was then driven from my lungs in a startled gasp I am awestruck and humbled by her radiance.

If the dream brings me happiness I rather live it than to stay awake,

You are my dream and I love every second of it you're my fantasy.

Confusions

Of

The Mind

Inside the shadow of I shifting eyes,
There stood a mirror reflecting not just I gaze,
But this perceptible uncertainty of I reality in disguise.
To I reflection I often ask, who am I?
Elegant, good order and enigmatic would be I reply.
Such an ostentatious description of self I cannot deny,
But this great feeling of the unknown is what I really want to pry.
I chant good fortune in I endeavours with an immaculate grin,
I inner voice tells I not to be ashamed of I abilities they'll be the impetus for I to win,
Losing isn't I fear,
Being a free thinker in this Matrix can be an emphatic sin.

It seems I & I been dealt by life an insoluble problem or something of the kind,
Bickered by turbulent frustrations and no one seems to have enough time.
In I head, there plays a well orchestrated music with such a beautiful chime,
The onus is now on I to vibrate at a higher frequency,
Just to relinquish this anguish of I unsettling Confusions of the Mind!

Converse

They say words are words used to define other words.
That kind of limitation is more than a vicious cycle, because there's so much to say but the words are sparse.
The molten moonlight pierces through my window and I am stuck in an enchanted gaze as insomnia grasps me in her ever waiting arms.
It's said that prayer is better than sleep, but doesn't God already know the state I'm in?
Now the illumination through my window is the sparkling Caribbean dawn slitting across the top of the hill. Here I sit in tumultuous silence trying to gather the rushing thoughts penetrating my mind.

.

Love, Sex, Money, Religion even Politics have all placed us all in a double bind;
That's a booming and dreary battle between the ego and I.

The truth is, I know the resolution for what I am going through so I should be fine.
There's so much I'd like to share with you it's like I hardly know anything about you at all,
Apart from you being a particularly luminous being,
I feel that we have a kind of kindred spirit afterall.
Through the labyrinths of my brain you often traverse,
And though the words are limited in this infinite world
It is such a joy whenever we converse.

Free On The Land

Wake up people the world is yours
Not being selfish the world is ours
You and I the division between first and second person is so shrewd
I & I the oneness within all that's me and you
It's such a joy to know we are all One
Just as corruption, greed, division and conflict are all the same cons
Ran by the Man;
Fractional Reserve Banking, Politics, Race and Religion are his very lucrative scams
It is really our innate duty now to eradicate his sisniter plan
Of total captivity of the only race on this Earth, Human
By simply living in love free on the land.

Hatred

The lips of many have uttered that hate is a very strong word.

Is that enough of a reason for me to conceal my apparent disdain?

You seem to reshuffle every organ in my body with these thoughts of you that keep dominating my mind against my will.

From my life you're gone and these sweet memories won't change a thing.

Heaven knows my contempt and how I cannot sacrifice anymore time on this, I thought with an inward sigh.

For you I am through, I sincerely have no more tears to cry.

I hate you I'm unsure but your actions I won't ever judge. Although I'm now stuck here in this valley I'll see it out since your love was merely a bitter refuge.

I hate everything about you, I do I swear!
I hate that I am fucking lying and for you I'll always care!
I hate that I am cognizant of the fact that I will love you till the time ends.
I hate that you've enchanted me with your Love, hatred's best friend!

I Ran Away

I have been feeling heavy-eyed and tired lately. I cannot seem to tell the difference between the days and the nights, my entire existence is engulfed in anxiety and pain. My agony drags on because I no longer know if it's worth fighting for.

My entire core now shivers, I am not properly equipped to handle this reality, and I'm not at all inured to this kind of tragedy.

I do not wish to be trapped in this aperture of uncertainty so I have to free myself, I have to escape, and I have to find a way!

Love?! I hope you hear me

My life had been grim in that valley, I felt pinned to the floor and I was swerving out of control.

Love, why are you so amazing and yet so cruel?

You were the only reason I stayed.

Now you can say I challenged you , that is why I Ran Away!

Identity
Crisis

Negroes, coloured, brown, black! All descriptions of the Melanin ones.
What's that?!
Sub-Human more like chattel they said,
But have failed to identify what is it we really lack.
Knowledge of self is the ultimate key,
Children of the Sun I hope these words allow you to see
No one is a colour! Let's trample that illusion!
The only way to claim our throne is when we see ourselves, together, robust and mighty as a Nation.
Negroes, coloured, brown, black! All descriptions of the Melanin ones.
What's that?!

The color of skin tone division made us poor and they gain from their unfair calculations, with no equality equity in their equations.
The world is unfair, aren't you tired of asking why that is?

We overstand it's just a sinister plot!
Recognize and rise above the travesty of mental slavery.
The only way to shed the burden of our identify crisis is to claim, embrace and highlight,
Our True Sovereignty!

In This Time

In this constant time
A time of an abundance of blessings
So much to be grateful for yet there is only one
day appointed for thanksgiving
Isn't this such a melancholic state we find
ouselves living in
Nothing seems to balance again
Even the meloday goes against the rhythm
Daily we give up our power
You desire to know of which power am I
speaking
That distinct one to resist this precarious
system!
A system propelled by hate, oppression,
prejudice
And all that negates the foudations of good
Our reality is now a world where its noble to
seek profit over personhood

I see a change on the horizon at the detriment of the high-horse riding few

The catalyst for this is because equilibrium for all is now being fully understood

Universial Love very much like the doctrine of salvation is free for us without a fine

Open that important closed eye and see the light

Our euphoric soul's liberation is totally attainable in the land of the living in this time

Isms

Material, Capital, Consumer, Class and Race!
Isms of the world leaving in the mouths of the
sun-kissed ones a bitter taste.
This Babylon system is such a waste
And if we perpetuate its cycle of continuity our
precious divinity we will replace
We won't be the fools who persisted in our
follies and gets wise
Rather we will be the fools ignorantly selling our
souls without a trace
Love and Compassion to us are naturally innate
But the aforementioned isms are the antonyms

Hate and Divisiveness they inflate
A soul liberation is for all of us to attain
Living sustainably and overcoming our shame
Rid these isms from your life this awesome
game
Indica and Sativa the cheat codes to rise
above this 3 Dimensional plane.

Love

Experience has taught me that wishful thinking only leads to disappointment.... But Love
Love is Strong as a Quietus
Jealousy is as cruel as a Catacomb

No waters cannot quench love
Neither can the floods drown it

It is spontaneous and craves our every expressions through joy, beauty, trust even tears. Love lives the moment, it's neither lost in the yesteryears nor ends, it craves for tomorrow. Love is now!
So as Macbeth asked, "Who could refrain,. That had a heart to love, and in that heart. Courage to make 's love known?"

Men Do Love

Being your slave, what shall I do but tend upon the hours and times of your desires.
But they say women are the victims and men are the perpetrators;

The psyche of our patriachal system is that women are the root of mankind's downfall. Programmed to blame, criticize, ridicule and belittle the Womb-Man, our mother of all creation.
The divine essence manifested in the physical realm as a Womb-Man, life's bundle of joy, happiness, compassion and pleasure. Only a real man can be fully aware of a Womb-Man's worth in the grand scheme of things, as she possesses the portal between the realms; he would be a martyr for his other half and is willing to be the victim as she is his treasure...

We should keep in mind that there is always some madness in love but there is always some reason in madness. With that said, men do love and it is more than a joy, it is the greatest pleasure!

Reminisce

Suddenly from somewhere behind me came a dreadful resonance.

I must be going crazy, since lately I have been stricken by hearing anomalous sounds.

There it goes again, and this time my frail heart gave a great jump so much so I bit my tongue to stop myself from screaming.

How do I face this apparent fear?

How do I overcome being worried that I am worried?

I shake my head dejectedly to how little one can foresee the future.

It was you! It has always been you and I knew it! You are my sensational torment! and the cause of this empathic noise creeping up on me whenever I am alone.

I sit in silence daily and long to know what is going to happen because the use of all my senses forcibly reminds me of you.
Your beautiful soul, the eloquence of your speech, the luminous spark of your stare; your entire being is to my mind every bit as fascinating as your sparkling red hair.

The
Affinity

Future is presented when its represented by the host of destiny, because destiny can be delayed but not denied...

The Affinity for this feeling, this feeling in your heart that is exposed, vulnerable, wonderful and awful, heart sick and alive at the same time. This feeling is Love.
Being in a state of inertia because this feeling won't ever leave you alone.
Love, a bare whisper that makes your body ignites with such uncontrollable curiosity.

In time we see that the Affinity for this feeling of Love is Life

The Bigger Picture

The world is staged and everyone has to play their role
Difficult it is living in this realm
The echoes quickers your being to become so cold
Genuine affection seems unattainble too
Bound to be the case with our trust openly bought and sold
Righteousness and oneness is our most desireable need
To overcome the real problematic epidemic of these times,
The vanity and our greed
Equality with International Morality for all is where we should approach

The Capitalistic system disguised as supply and demand is affecting our souls
Driven by profit we've slowly become their ghosts
Creating the poverty that feeds the destruction the most
To our renaissane resistance I propose a toast
To the Bigger Picture!
And that's the greater good for all of course

The Bliss Of Love

I say Knowledge is pain. The tragedy of sexual intercourse is the perpetual virginity of the soul, thus a sense of love, the feeling or the ability is needed.

I've realized and accepted that even between the closest of partners, infinite distances and differences continue to exist; I've succeeded in loving these distances and differences between us now I can see you whole against the sky. I say life without love is like a tree without blossoms or fruit, because just as how the Godhead is not an object of its own knowledge, love has no desire but to fulfil itself, to be like a running brook that sings its melody to the night, to wake at dawn with a winged heart and give thanks for another day of loving, its like tasting hot chocolate before its cool, first it takes you by surprise but keeps you warm for a long time.

Love, a symbol of eternity. Its wipes out all sense of time, destroying all memory of a beginning and all fear of an end.

That is The Bliss of Love, are you able to experience this feeling?

Third World

There's this place that's...
Systematically underdeveloped because of greed.
We cry for equal rights and justice as if those values aren't an universal creed.
We beg for only just a slice of the cake,
While we ignorantly ignore we are the bakers in the bakery known as the state.
Our struggles are robustly real but we can't afford to ever be faint.
Because...
Opportunities seem rare and can even seem very microscopic,
Small talks are useless unless hustling for better is the topic;
Aspirations to overcome explains the fighting spirit we exhibit.
Though...

From the poverty and pressure there's no place to hide
It's not our choice but in the belly of the beast we reside,
With that said where we're from doesn't affect our self-worth coupled with our pride.
That's why....
We live against all odds with an outlook on life that's postive,
Yes, so much trouble in our little world
Yet we are so very happy fundamentally, in this Third World we live.

Unbreakable

Lessons taught from wrangling with life must be learnt,
And in all strife no bridges should be burnt.
Preparation for greatness comes with a plethora of battles to fight,
Endurance in this race is the truest testament of might.
Claiming and clinging to a personality is merely just a perception,
To be aligned with growth is mastering yourself close to perfection.
How is that done in this life we all live? Doesn't it feel like an illusion? Sure, yes it is!
And for continuously lying to ourselves we all must forgive.
The answer to all our prayers is to live life and let love live.
What do you do for a living?
Is a very repulsive question everyone should love to hate!

Careers are now our lives,
No wonder why most of us are trapped in this routine zombie like state.
Let us live for a living and execute our paradigm shift,
It is the way of waking up if you caught my drift.
The 5th Dimensional God Consciousness is totally attainable,
Open your Eye from its slumber and truly become,
UNBREAKABLE!

Printed in Great Britain
by Amazon

65905071R00030